"Let Me Try"

MAZES

PRESCHOOL FUNBOOK

CREATIVE CHILD PRESS ® is a registered trademark of Playmore Inc., Publishers and Waldman Publishing Corp., New York, New York

Published by Playmore Inc., Publishers and Waldman Publishing Corp., New York, New York

TO THE PARENT

Solving mazes has always been a favorite activity of children. Now the fun is within the reach of even younger preschoolers with this wonderful collection of specially designed mazes that are bold and big enough for use with jumbo crayons, and wide markers, suitable for even the smallest hands.

These mazes are delightful drawings of objects that children are familiar with. Making them into mazes makes them even more fun! At the same time, solving each one gives the child a sense of accomplishment and pride.

"Let Me Try!" That's what every child wants to do. These delightful MAZES will enable your child to try — and succeed!

Penny's Path

Help Penny find her missing blocks!

Birthday Bike

Help Tony reach his brand new bike!

Frankie Frog

Show Frankie the way to munch
through the melon!

Sunshine Surprise

Breeze through this sunny maze!

Ten-Gallon Search

Can you find your way through the cowboy hat?

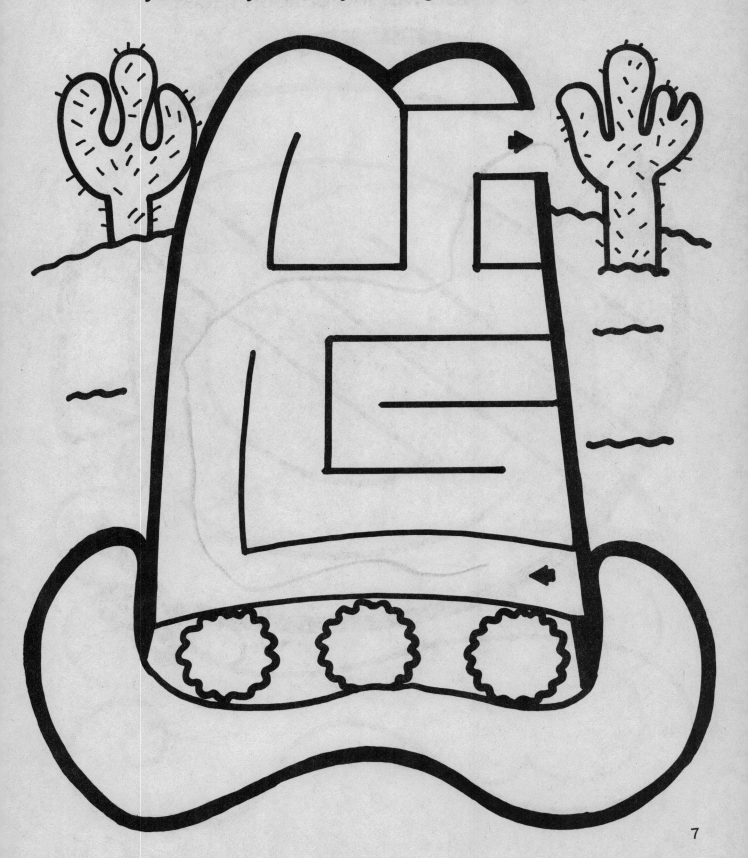

Big Balloon

Can you win the balloon race?

Mushroom Maze

Wriggle your way through this one!

Benny Bird

Help Benny peck his way through
the strawberry!

Clyde the Clam

Help Clyde glide to Sally Starfish!

I Lost My Way!

Can you help the little bird find his way home?

Happy Hive

Help the queen bee out of this hive!

The Witch's Brew

Help Piggy Witch find her pot of brew!

Pasture Puzzle

Lead Millie Mare out of the pasture!

Veggie Venture

Help the chef find the veggies for his stew!

Train Trail

Can the engine find his runaway caboose?

Wacky Wheels

Drive through this wacky maze!

Tea Time

Can you whistle your way through?

Hurried Hamster

He can spin his way out!

Cracked Crown

A royal maze!

Missing Puppy

Help Patty find her lost puppy!

Lily Lamb

Hurry! Start at the B and come out of the A!

23

It's In The Bag

Find your way to the lunch at the bottom of the bag.

24

Party Puzzle

Pop in and out of the party hat!

Castle Puzzle

Trapped! Can you find your way
out of the castle?

Add It Up

Calculate how to escape!

Happy Halloween

Can you find the missing candy?

Hot Dog Hoopla

Hot dog wants to find mustard and ketchup.
Can you help?

Benny Beaver

Lead Benny to the tasty tree!

Berry Bush

Find your way through the bushes!

Hectic Haystacks

Crunch your way through this one!

Popcorn Maze

Nibble your way through!

Brooke's Baby

Help Brooke find her baby doll!

Luke's Lollipop

Can Luke reach his lucky lollipop?

Bonnie's Buggy

Help Bonnie Doll find her way out of the buggy!

Flag Fun

Unfurl your way through this one!

Giant Globe

Spin your way through this maze!

River Rhino

Find the right path through Richie Rhino!

Clever Cat

Start with the M and come out at the W!

Pig Out

Lead the pigs to their dinner!

Moo-ve It

Start at the M and come out the O!

Genie Jumble

Rub your way through the magic lamp!

Whale Of A Maze

Work your way through Wally Whale!

Banana Maze

Peel your way through this slippery one!

Picnic Prize

Which ant will reach the picnic basket?

Billy Bat

Wing your way out of this one!

Tropical Trail

Sail your way to the island!

Super Skate

Speed your way through the maze!

Toucan Tina

Fly through this maze!

Pie Puzzle

Chomp your way in and out of the delicious pie!

Wise Guy

Show the owl how to get from H to T!

Mousehole Maze

Can you help Marty Mouse find the right path?

Ornament Fun

Can you find your way through the ornament?

Cozy Coat

Start at one glove and come out the other!

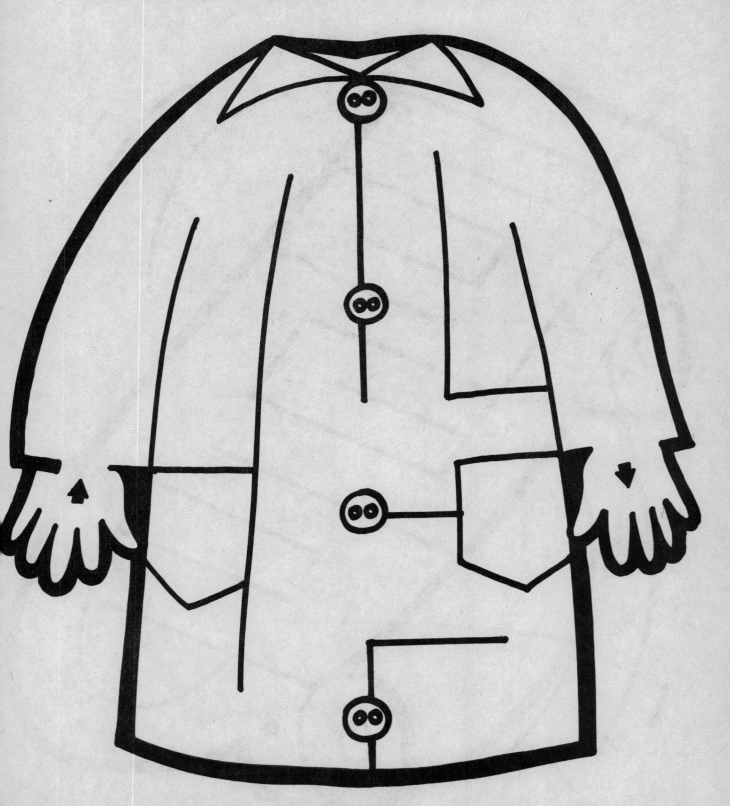

Skateboard Maze

Speed your way through this one!

Giddy Ghost

Lead the ghost through the haunted house!

Sea Serpent Search

Find a path through the monster!

Gary Gopher

Help Gary tunnel his way out!

Pretty Purse

Find your way to the set of keys!

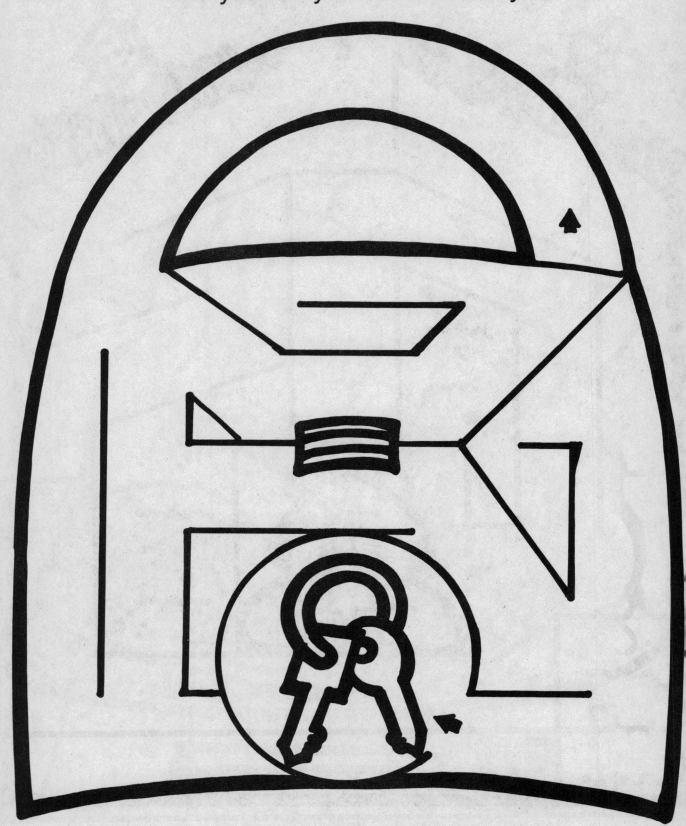

Silly Spaghetti

Can you find a path through the noodles?

Busy Book

Can you find your way through the pages?

Mailbox Maze

Help the letter get in and out of the mailbox!

Buzzing By

Start with the B and come out the Z!

Tricky Tube

Help the toothpaste come out the
other end of the tube!

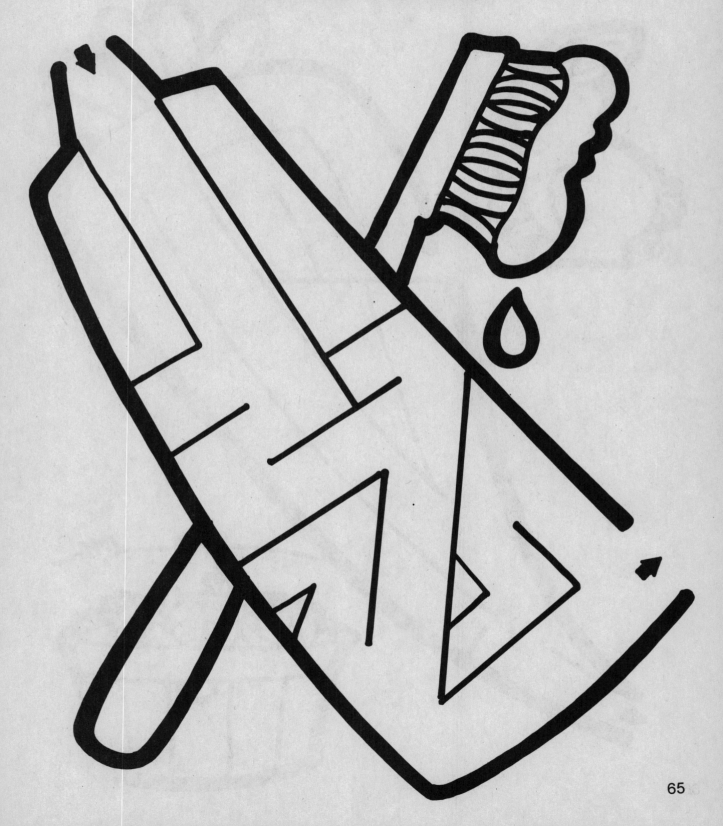

Crazy Carrot

Can Rodney Rabbit munch his way
through the carrot?

Rock the Cradle

Find the way out of the cradle!

Brenda Bunny

Quick! Get Brenda to her umbrella!

Daring Deer

Dart this deer in and out of the maze!

Diane Duck

Diane needs your help to find her baby duckling!

Eager Eagle

Get the eagle to the top of the cliff!

Clown Car

Get Clarence to his car!

Delightful Dancer

Bring Heather Hippo to her ballet shoes!

Sneaky Snake

Slither through the H and come out the S!

Caught in the Corn

Lead the crow out of the cornfield!

Splendid Slope

Get Bart down the slope fast!

Plenty of Plants

Lead the hungry dino to some delicious plants!

Lots of Work

Help Elmer Elf find Santa's workshop!

Chasing Champ

Follow Champ to his dog dish!

Water Can Wonder

Wander through the water!

Rowdy Race

Which car will get to the finish line?

Freddie Frog

Start at the H and end at the P!

Get the Gift

Find the path to the present inside!

Bernie Bunny

Hop to it to solve this one!

Egg-citing Maze

Help the baby chick find her way out!

Treasure Trail

Can you find the hidden treasure?

Pool Puzzle

Find the way through the pool!

Bubble Bath

Start at the top and go out the bottom!

88

Baffled Bear

Help the bear out of his den!

Purring Puzzle

Find a way through Katie Kitty!

Prickly Puzzle

Don't get stuck!

Gloria Goat

Help Gloria reach the can!

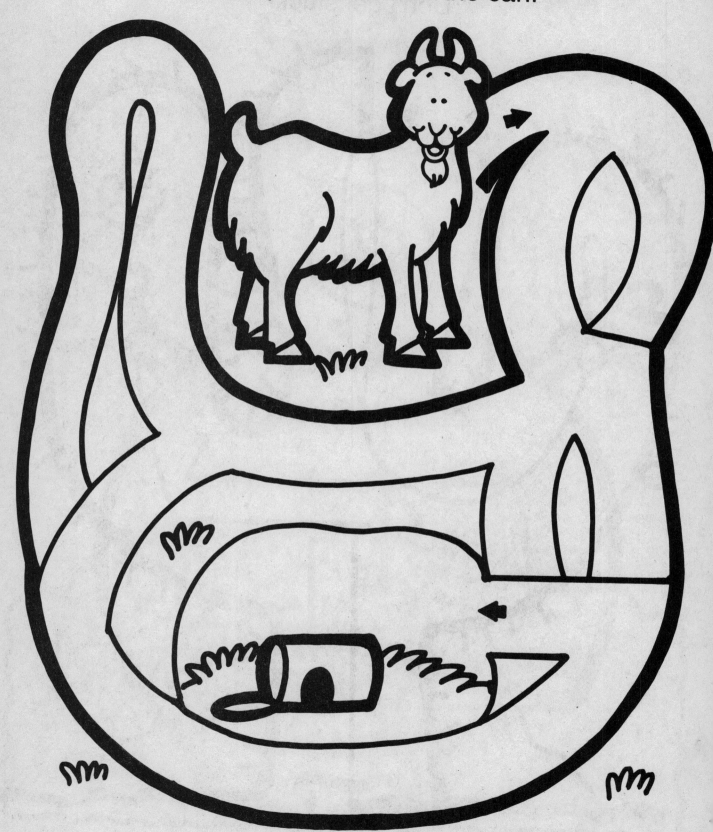

Sam Snowman

How fast can you get through this one?

Big Bark

Start at the R and come out the F.

Lighted Lamp

Find your way out of this little lamp!

Gilda Goldfish

Help Gilda to the bottom of the fishbowl!

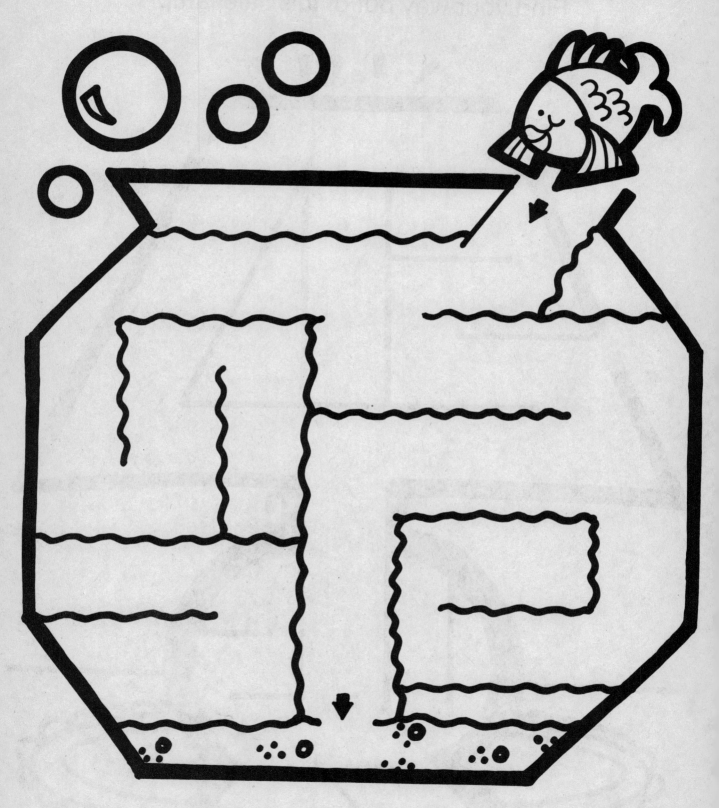

SOLUTIONS

page 3

page 4

page 5

page 6

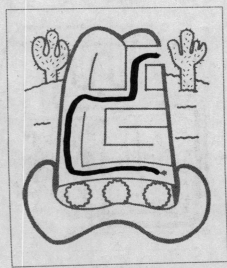

page 7

page 8

page 9

page 10

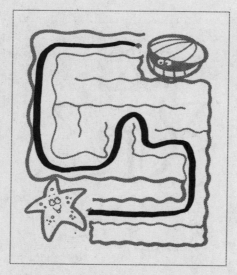

page 11

page 12

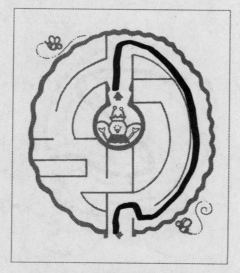

page 13

page 14

page 15

page 16

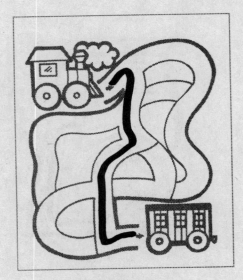

page 17

page 18

page 19

page 20

page 21

page 22

page 23

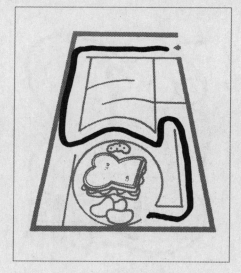

page 24

page 25

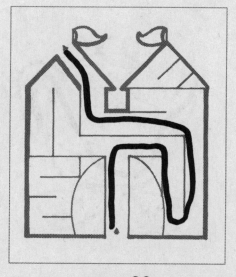

page 26

page 27

page 28

page 29

page 30

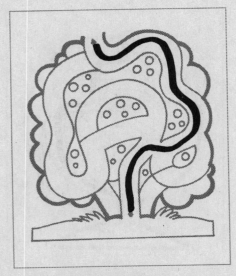

page 31

page 32

page 33

page 34

page 35

page 36

page 37

page 38

page 39

page 40

page 41

page 42

page 43

page 44

page 45

page 46

page 47

page 48

page 49

page 50

page 51

page 52

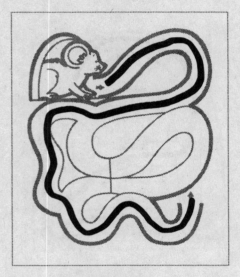

page 53

page 54

page 55

page 56

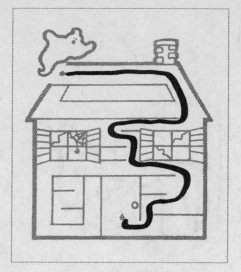

page 57

page 58

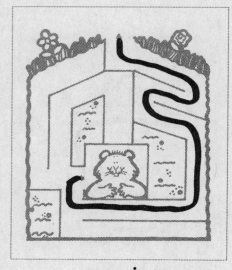

page 59

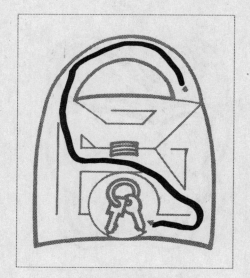

page 60

page 61

page 62

page 63

page 64

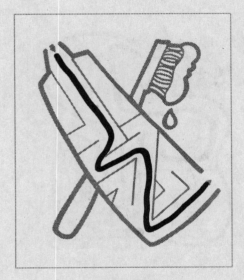

page 65

page 66

page 67

page 68

page 69

page 70

page 71

page 72

page 73

page 74

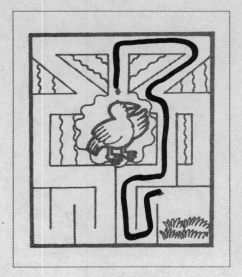

page 75

page 76

page 77

page 78

page 79

page 80

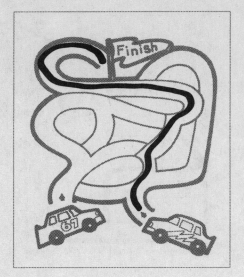

page 81

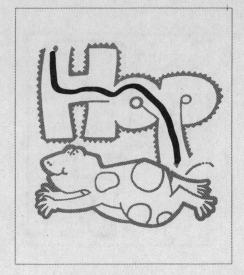

page 82

page 83

page 84

page 85

page 86

page 87

page 88

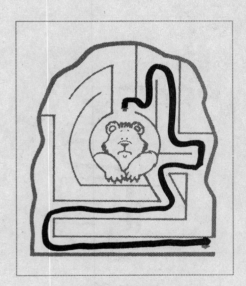

page 89

page 90

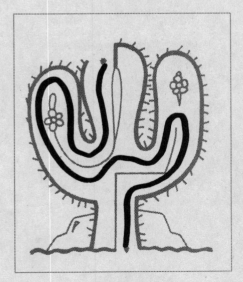

page 91

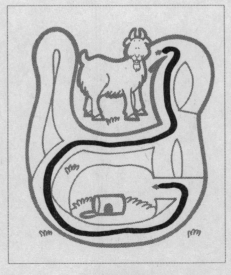

page 92

page 93

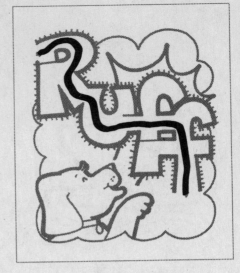

page 94

page 95

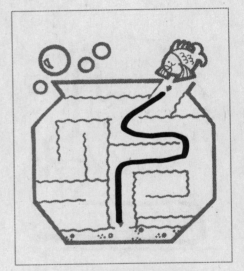

page 96